D1073944

This library edition published in 2011 by Walter Foster Publishing, Inc.
Walter Foster Library
Distributed by Black Rabbit Books
P.O. Box 3263 Mankato, Minnesota 56002

Printed in China, Shanghai Offset Printing Products Limited, Shenzhen.

First Library Edition

Library of Congress Cataloging-in-Publication Data

Wright, Diane.
  Beautiful landscapes / by Diane Wright. -- 1st library ed.
     p. cm. -- (Drawing made easy)
  ISBN 978-1-936309-11-5 (hardcover)
  1. Landscape drawing--Technique. 2. Pencil drawing--Technique. I. Title.
  NC795.W75 2011
  743'.836--dc22

                                                        2010005322

022010
0P1815

9 8 7 6 5 4 3 2 1

DRAWING
MADE
EASY

BEAUTIFUL LANDSCAPES

By Diane Wright

www.walterfoster.com

CONTENTS

INTRODUCTION

I am often asked why I draw barns. I live in the heart of the Midwest and was raised on a family farm, so rural landscapes are a part of who I am. The Midwestern landscape is riddled with old barns and farmhouses, icons of an era in American history when life was simpler, days were spent working the land, and families formed the core of each farm. I am proud to say I was a part of that era, and my passion for my surroundings is evident in my drawings. Discovering a passion for your subject matter is the first step in expressing yourself through art. Really observe the scenery around you; take a child's viewpoint and see anew. Drawing what you see every day is so important—all those underlying feelings can't help but be reflected in your artwork.

The next step in learning to create art is choosing a medium. I use graphite pencil for my finished artwork—it is simple and direct and an incredible tool for artistic expression. The pencil is an extension of the hand, and the flow to the paper is seamless. Effective use of value and textures can evoke as much color and drama as any painting. The black-and-white graphite medium also has a timeless quality to it. The process of drawing provides learning opportunities, appreciation for the wealth of detail in the world, and a feeling of personal connection to a landscape. I love what I can achieve with just a pencil.

Drawing landscapes can seem intimidating, but it becomes much easier by breaking down each element into separate, more manageable tasks. Before you know it, a landscape will unfold before your eyes. The goal of this book is to review each aspect of drawing landscapes, one step at a time. By sharing my personal approach and techniques with you, we are going to explore creating beautiful landscapes together. The world is ready and waiting to be drawn.

TOOLS AND MATERIALS

Graphite pencil is the simplest art medium. All you really need are a drawing surface, pencil, and paper. But a selection of tools can make drawing more fun and results more professional. Here are some tools that I find useful; try various materials and see what works best for you.

Workspace Good lighting is essential for drawing, and natural lighting is always a bonus! Northern exposure provides the most natural light and is the best to work by. I supplement the natural lighting in my studio with two clamp lamps with daylight or full-spectrum bulbs. These provide bright, white light and eliminate the yellow glare typical of standard bulbs. You can draw on your kitchen table or desk, but a large drafting table (as shown in the photo) makes a world of difference. I keep a tray to the left of the table to hold pencils, erasers, and rulers. Two plastic storage bins below the table hold extra supplies. A long, angled piece of drawing paper clamped onto the table functions as a paper shield, protecting my drawing paper from smudges and skin oils. There is plenty of room on the table to tape several reference photos. (I do not tape my drawing paper down while I draw; instead, I angle the paper or even turn it upside down.)

Choosing Paper Not all papers provide the same results. Sketch-pads are just for that—sketching! If you are going to invest your time in creating finished works of art, invest in high-quality, acid-free paper produced especially for drawing. Bristol paper, which comes in pads or individual sheets, is an excellent choice. It is available with either a smooth plate finish (which I use for the projects in this book) or a textured vellum finish. Smooth-finish Bristol paper has a very slight texture that is excellent for graphite pencil work; it allows for great detail and dark, rich values.

Transferring an Image

It's a good idea to start your drawings on a piece of tracing vellum so you can rework and refine the drawing before transferring it to your final art paper. Tracing vellum is a heavyweight, translucent paper that withstands heavy erasing. (Tracing vellum is different from vellum-finish Bristol paper.) When you're satisfied with your initial drawing, turn over the tracing vellum and cover the back with an even coat of graphite. Then

place the vellum on top of your art paper, graphite-side down. Trace over the lines you want to keep with a hard 2H pencil. The pressure of your pencil will transfer the lines to the art paper below. (Another method involves transfer paper, which is a sheet of paper coated on one side with graphite. Simply place one sheet—graphite-side down—between the tracing vellum and art paper before you trace. You also may prefer to transfer images using the grid method—see page 29.) Occasionally lift the corner the tracing vellum (and the transfer paper, if applicable) to make sure the lines are transferring correctly. After transferring, clean up the drawing with an eraser.

Pencils Pencil "lead" (actually graphite) comes in varying degrees of hardness. Soft leads produce dense, black marks, and hard leads produce lighter marks. Soft leads are labeled with a number and a B (for "black") and hard leads with a number and an H (for "hard"). The higher the number, the harder or softer the lead. HB and F are used for the middle grades. My mainstay is a mechanical pencil with a .5 mm lead. The thinner .3 mm lead is useful for adding detail in the smallest areas. A *clutch pencil* is similar to a mechanical pencil, but it holds only a thicker 2mm lead, which is ideal for broad strokes. I use the full range of mechanical pencil leads (6H–4B) available and keep a handful of 8H–6H and 5B–9B wooden pencils for rare occasions when I need extremely soft or hard leads.

Erasers I think of an eraser more as a drawing tool than as a tool for removing mistakes. Often I will apply graphite heavily to an area with the intent of coming back and lightening it with an eraser. This can create subtle, controlled highlights and textures. In addition to the traditional erasers, I use adhesive putty, made for tacking posters to a wall. (I call it a "tacky eraser.") I can mold it into different shapes, just like a kneaded eraser, and it won't ruin the drawing surface. A battery-operated eraser also is a wonderful tool. To avoid smearing or damaging the paper, first lift off as much graphite as possible using a tacky eraser; then use the battery-powered eraser.

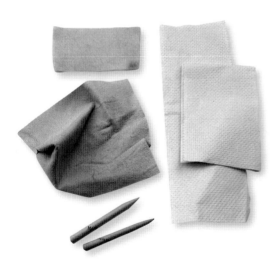

Blending Tools Blending tools can be used to create a variety of effects. I use blending most frequently when drawing skies. A chamois creates the smoothest and most even blending. Felt is great for textured paper. Paper towels also work for general blending, and *tortillons* (tightly wound sticks of paper pointed at one end) can be used for smaller areas.

Extras A number of additional tools help me maintain and make the best use of my drawing tools and protect my drawing surface. For drawing straight lines or checking angles, I use a T square or a ruler. To lightly brush away eraser crumbs and excess graphite, I dust the drawing with a make-up brush. (Never use your hand or blow on your drawing surface!) I use a sandpaper block to create chisel points on pencil leads or fine points on erasers, and I sometimes use an eraser shield for lifting out tone in specific shapes. I also spray workable fixative on completed drawings to protect them from smearing.

PENCIL TECHNIQUES

You can create a variety of effects with a pencil—from soft, painterly blends and loose, carefree lines to firm, deliberate strokes and tight, precise details. The way you grip the pencil, the pressure you apply, and the directions of your strokes all affect your results. Experiment with the different hand positions and techniques shown here; the more you practice, the better you will be able to manipulate the pencil to the desired effect.

▶ **Underhand Grip** This position provides a wonderfully loose and flowing pencil stroke. Hold your palm above and almost parallel to the drawing surface with the pencil running under and across your palm. Keeping your wrist stiff, use your entire arm to make the stroke. An excellent exercise is to stand a full arm's length away from a piece of sketch paper clipped to a board leaned on an easel and practice making long, fluid pencil strokes.

◀ **Loose-Hold Grip** I like to use this position when drawing light, straight lines for large areas, such as the base layer of a sky (see page 19). Holding the pencil loosely between your thumb and first two fingers, let the weight of the pencil control the weight of the pencil stroke.

▶ **Writing Grip** This is the most comfortable position— the same position you use for writing. It provides more control for detailed areas. To create a more fluid motion and pencil stroke, keep your wrist stiff and avoid resting your wrist or hand on the paper.

Hatching This is the most direct way to apply a layer of graphite. Simply draw a series of parallel lines. The closer you place the parallel strokes, the darker the value will be.

Crosshatching This technique, which I use most often, involves layering closely spaced hatch marks, with each layer hatched in a different direction. The more layers, the darker the value.

Blending For a smooth, blended texture, use the loose-hold grip to create light, crosshatched layers. Then wrap a piece of chamois around your index finger and use a light, circular motion to blend the lines together.

Scribbling This technique creates an ideal texture for leaves and bushes. Hold the pencil in the underhand grip and make small, controlled scribbles. Increasing the pressure produces darker values. Layers of scribbles result in an even texture.

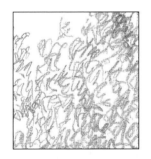

Burnishing For a smooth, slick look, apply a harder lead over a softer lead. For example, start with a soft 2B lead to lay down initial details (near right). Then "burnish" over the area with a 6H (far right). For an uneven texture that's ideal for rocks and bricks, reverse and burnish a hard lead with a soft lead.

Drawing Practices to Avoid

1. *Using a lead that is too hard.*
It is better to start with a lead that may be too soft (B to 2B) than one that may be too hard (2H or harder). If the lead is too hard, it is difficult and sometimes impossible to develop dark shading. Softer leads are more grainy by nature, but by going back and burnishing with a harder lead, you can achieve deep, rich values.

2. *Not making values dark enough.*
Use the full range of values (see pages 9–10) at your disposal. Without punched-up darks, your drawing will lack the desired impact.

3. *Being too timid.*
If you are hesitant with your pencil stroke, your drawing will reflect it. Be confident and sure of your intent *before* putting your pencil to the paper. Preplanning and practicing on another paper will assist greatly.

4. *Overworking.*
Keep your artwork fresh. Work out problem areas on tracing or scrap paper instead of erasing and redrawing on the real artwork.

Drawing Practices to Follow

When learning to draw, remember the three Ps: patience, practice, and perseverance. Be patient with yourself. Practice, practice, and practice some more. Perseverance will carry you through the challenges you'll encounter along the way.

Circular Motion
When you don't want visible directional strokes, make small, circular strokes. This creates even values and works great in dark, shadowed areas. Varying the pressure controls the darkness or lightness of the texture.

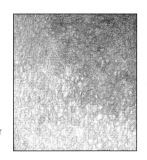

DRAWING BASICS

Although many folks consider my artwork detailed and realistic, I actually consider my drawings to be *representational*. I strive for a realistic feel, but the textures and pencil strokes only give the illusion of realism. In much of my artwork, the pencil stroke actually can be seen. In more realistic approaches, the pencil stroke would not be so easily detected. As an example, I strive to give the *impression* of tree leaves, not to draw the individual leaves. I provide just enough clues for the viewer to interpret the various landscape elements.

The representational approach offers the freedom to use interpretive pencil strokes to create textures. I have the flexibility to provide detail where I want and leave secondary or supportive areas out of focus. The result is a fresh, spontaneous composition.

Regardless of whether your approach is sketchy, representational, or ultrarealistic, there are four important elements that help create the illusion of reality: outline, light and shadow, texture, and perspective. You can manipulate these elements to provide your drawings with the appearance of three-dimensionality. Read on to find out how!

Outline

The inherent and most basic nature of a pencil is that it produces a line of graphite when applied to paper. A line can be extremely expressive and represent depth by the mere pressure applied as it is drawn. But things don't really have lines around them, so outlines should not be used to represent shapes or forms. Strong outlines will diminish the realistic quality of a drawing. The fewer the visible lines in your drawing, the more realistic your drawing will become.

Seeing Value and Texture As you can see in this photo, the shapes that make up the barrel are defined by shifts in value and texture—not by bold outlines. Although outlines will help you establish basic shapes in your initial sketch, minimize them as the drawing progresses.

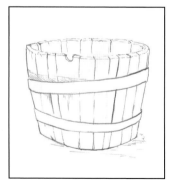

Outline Only In this first rendering of a barrel, I use only outline to represent the object. To avoid making the barrel completely flat and uninteresting, I express depth by altering the weight of the outline.

Shading for Depth I apply shading in this version, but the outlines are still too heavy and intrusive, lessening the realism of the barrel.

Minimizing Lines This illustration uses the most realistic approach: The outlines have been minimized, allowing light and shadow, as well as texture, to define the form of the object realistically.

Light and Shadow

Because graphite creates only shades of gray, *value* (the relative lightness or darkness of the graphite) is all we have to represent light and shadow in pencil drawings. Value is our most effective and expressive tool. Remember that there will always be at least one light source; otherwise, the object would be completely black. There are four main components of light and shadow: *highlights,* where the strongest light directly hits the surface of the object; *midtones,* where light indirectly hits the surface; *reflected light,* where light bounces back onto the object; and *shadows,* where light is blocked from the surface. *Core shadows* (also called "form" shadows) are those on the object itself; they are the darkest and strongest shadows. *Cast shadows* are those that an object throws onto other surfaces; they vary in value, depending on the light source.

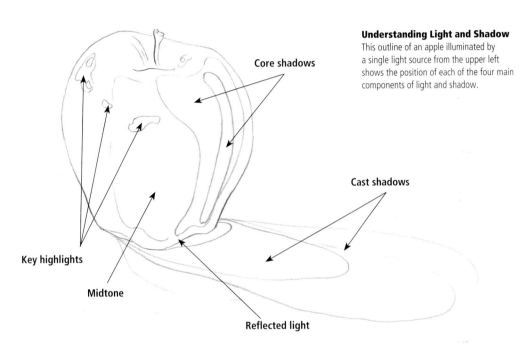

Core shadows

Cast shadows

Key highlights

Midtone

Reflected light

Understanding Light and Shadow
This outline of an apple illuminated by a single light source from the upper left shows the position of each of the four main components of light and shadow.

Applying Light and Shadow This completed drawing shows that the midtone values are relatively dark and are close in value to the darkest shadowed areas. We know it is a Red Delicious apple because of its shape and dark, varied values. We can almost see that it is red. The light and shadows define the apple's three-dimensional form. Imagine the coloring of a green Granny Smith apple and consider how you would draw it differently to depict its lighter coloring and rounder shape.

Understanding the Use of Values

When observing a landscape, you must be able to evaluate it in terms of values and learn how to use the values effectively in your drawings. If all the elements of a scene are too close in value, the landscape will be monotonous. But if the full spectrum of values is used in every element, the landscape will have no continuity, and the viewer won't know where to look. Careful value planning is the key to creating dynamic scenes. Experiment with changing the values in a scene, such as placing the foreground object in shadow and the background in direct light—or vice versa. It is up to you, the artist, to decide where you want the emphasis to be and what effect you want to achieve.

Additionally, always look for opportunities to explore unusual lighting and creative shadowing in landscapes. A unique "play of light" adds drama and contrast to a drawing. So, when drawing outdoors, remember that early morning and late afternoon lighting will produce the longest and most interesting cast shadows.

Using a Value Scale A good guideline to follow is that every landscape drawing should include at least six values spanning both ends of the spectrum—from the white of the paper to the darkest (almost black) dark.

Hand-Drawn Scale Different pencil brands, types, and lead hardnesses will produce different value ranges. A hand-drawn value scale is important for learning what values your pencils can produce.

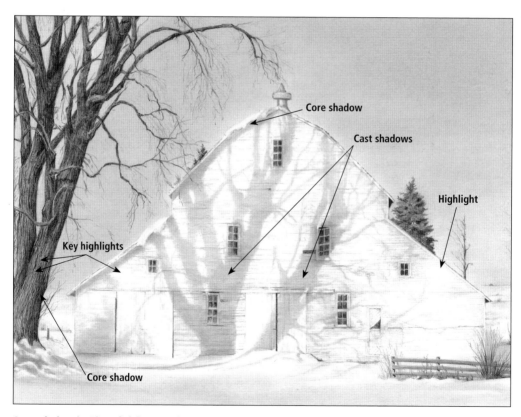

Appreciating the Play of Light Notice that the tree's cast shadow dancing across the face of the barn plays an important role in the success of this landscape.

Texture

The concepts of light, shadow, and texture are closely related. You have to understand the effects of light and shadow to create the illusion of texture in a drawing. By cleverly applying highlights (light) and shading (shadows), you can depict any texture—from rough wood and craggy rocks to wispy grasses and rippling waters.

Smooth, shiny surfaces like metal or glass have little or no texture, so the pencil strokes should be as smooth and fine as possible. The highlights and shadows on smooth surfaces generally have sharp, distinct edges. On the other hand, rough textures, such as rusted metal or certain types of rocks, are dull with small pits in the surface. As light hits each of the small pits, a tiny cast shadow is thrown, so the pencil strokes should be irregular with varying values. Highlights and shadows on rough surfaces generally have softer, more indefinite edges.

Wood

Although it is tempting to use the blending method to get an even-toned value, it is not the best way. Remember that blending will dissolve any details that we have worked so hard to develop. There is a better way. Using the burnishing method to create the illusion of wood grain creates amazing results.

Burnishing For the first layer, use a 2H lead and vertical strokes. To create the second layer, use an F lead to draw the horizontal lines of the grain, as well as knots and nail holes. Finally, use a 6H lead to burnish an even layer of tone over the first two layers. Add details as needed and lift out highlights using a tacky eraser.

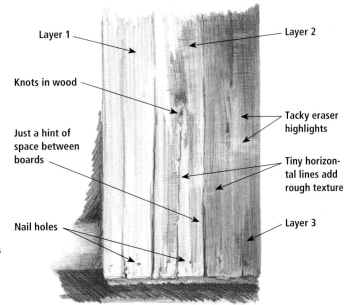

Layer 1

Layer 2

Knots in wood

Tacky eraser highlights

Just a hint of space between boards

Tiny horizontal lines add rough texture

Nail holes

Layer 3

Rocks

Reducing the forms of rocks to their most basic shapes—rectangle, circle, or triangle—will give you a perfect base to build on. You can then "morph" the shapes into angular planes and indicate reflected light and cast shadows for depth.

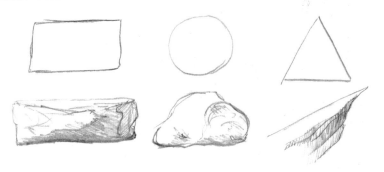

Identifying Basic Shapes This rock cluster is much easier to create once I have determined that the basic shape of the rock is round.

Grass

With some experimentation and practice, you can achieve effective results when drawing grass. By creating multiple layers, you can achieve a sense of depth. Here are four points to consider: (1) Draw the shadows behind the grass to quickly create distant grass. Just suggest the grass with a few spikes. (2) When drawing foreground grass, provide enough detail to keep the viewer's interest without drawing every single blade. Showing spaces between the weeds and overlapping the layers helps create foreground grass. (3) Use different textures to depict various species of grass and weeds. Introducing a few broadleaf weeds among bunches of long grass can add variety and interest. (4) The direction in which weeds are drawn is an effective and subtle way of leading the viewer's eye through the drawing and can really bring a whole scene together. Never let your weeds point out of the picture plane, as this will also lead the eye right out of the picture.

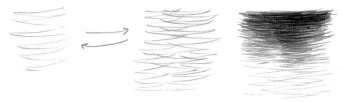

Grass Use layers of vertical pencil strokes to show patches of long grass. Pay careful attention not to create a single line of grass. Working from back to front and drawing the shadows between just the tips of the weeds creates a flowing patch.

Water

By overlaying horizontal pencil strokes, you quickly can create an effective representation of still water. Exaggerating the rocking motion suggests waves. Add more layers with defined highlights to show reflections in the water.

Creating the Feel of Motion Use a horizontal, back-and-forth stroke to depict moving water.

Contrasting Textures

This rendering of a brick wall is a good example of contrasting textures in a composition. The slick, smooth texture of the window nicely contrasts the rough texture of the bricks. I use the circular motion and burnishing to create the rich, even texture for the window, and I use reverse burnishing to create the uneven texture of the bricks. By emphasizing the extremes of texture, the brick wall takes on a dramatic, sun-baked atmosphere.

Perspective

Perspective helps create the illusion and sense of depth and distance in drawings. Understanding and correctly applying the rules of perspective to your drawings will lend them a higher degree of realism. *Linear perspective* makes use of the illusion that parallel lines converge as they grow more distant. *Aerial perspective* is the use of reduced size and lighter, less defined imagery to represent distant objects. The first step in applying the rules of perspective to a scene is to find the horizon line. It might be below or above the actual horizon, depending on your vantage point. From there you establish a *vanishing point,* the point where receding parallel lines seem to converge on the horizon. *One-point perspective* means that you have only a single vanishing point. *Two-point perspective* employs two vanishing points, which often sit off the picture plane to the far right and left. For more information, see William F. Powell's book *Perspective* (AL13) in Walter Foster's Artist's Library series.

One-Point Perspective The railroad tracks converge at a single vanishing point on the horizon. (Notice that the foliage also becomes smaller and less detailed in the distance.)

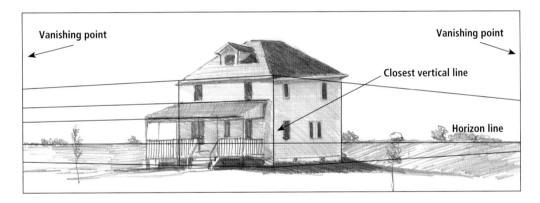

Two-Point Perspective In the first drawing of a house in an open field, it is easy to see that the angle of the roof is wrong based on the guidelines leading to the vanishing points. On closer analysis, the front of the house is also angled incorrectly, as well as the porch roofline. (A common mistake is having the windows not leading to the same point as the roofline.) Compare the first illustration with the second one. See how the second house "sits" on the paper and gives an appropriate sense of depth.

DRAWING TREES AND FOLIAGE

Trees and foliage are some of the most challenging and complex objects to draw—but nothing can add more expression, mood, and life to a drawing. Combining our philosophy of practice, patience, and perseverance with the drawing basics covered on pages 8–13 will give you the stepping stones to explore and draw the awesome beauty of trees. It's important to study trees and understand their differences before drawing them, so use the examples on the next five pages to become comfortable with depicting these essential aspects of landscapes.

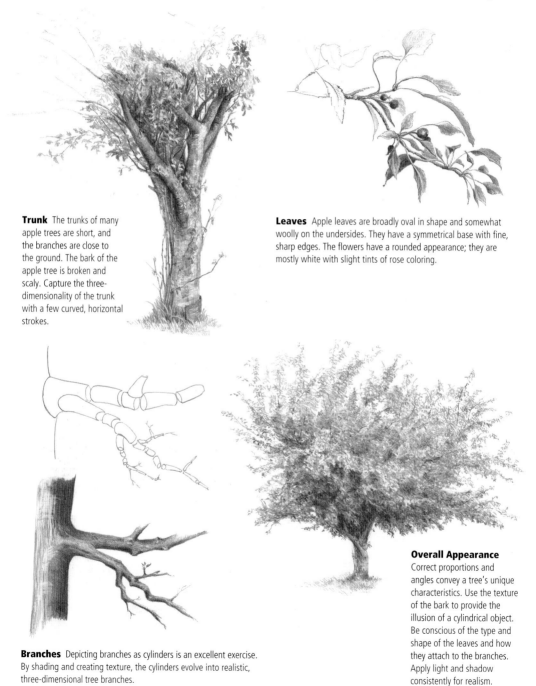

Trunk The trunks of many apple trees are short, and the branches are close to the ground. The bark of the apple tree is broken and scaly. Capture the three-dimensionality of the trunk with a few curved, horizontal strokes.

Leaves Apple leaves are broadly oval in shape and somewhat woolly on the undersides. They have a symmetrical base with fine, sharp edges. The flowers have a rounded appearance; they are mostly white with slight tints of rose coloring.

Branches Depicting branches as cylinders is an excellent exercise. By shading and creating texture, the cylinders evolve into realistic, three-dimensional tree branches.

Overall Appearance Correct proportions and angles convey a tree's unique characteristics. Use the texture of the bark to provide the illusion of a cylindrical object. Be conscious of the type and shape of the leaves and how they attach to the branches. Apply light and shadow consistently for realism.

◀ **Grounding a Tree** If the tree you are drawing doesn't have a solid foundation, it will look like it is floating on the paper. So how do you plant the tree firmly in the ground? Here are some tips: (1) Draw grass around the roots and behind the tree; (2) use shading to develop the form; (3) flange out the base of the tree; and (4) show parts of the roots.

▶ **Tree Anatomy** Drawing a bare winter tree is an excellent way to learn the anatomy of a tree. Pay particular attention to how each limb attaches to the trunk, each branch to its limb, and each twig to its branch. A common mistake in drawing branches is to make them too straight. Details like knots, kinks, and bends add life. Observe the spaces between the branches and follow every branch through. Don't let a branch grow out of nowhere or at an unrealistic angle.

Pinecone

Pine Trees Pines are distinctive trees with needles, cones, and unique shaping. Pine trees have a natural, calming effect and make great supporting backgrounds for landscapes.

Pine needles

Capturing the Essence

The term "strength" best expresses the large, solid, and robust stature of oak trees. There are many spaces between branches, which make it easier to study the armature (structure). In this tree study, I exaggerate and accentuate the unique curvature of the main trunk with special attention to the flow of the branches, emphasizing and de-emphasizing areas to complement and show off Mother Nature's handiwork. After carefully sketching the branches with all their intricate curves, I use a 4B lead to boldly draw them with one stroke. I add the small leaf bundles with the scribble method, keeping them close to the trunk.

Oak Tree Leaf Oak leaves are long, tapered at the base, and cut into lobes on each side. In this leaf study, I indent the fine leaf veins into the paper using the metal tip of a mechanical pencil with the lead retracted. (A dull darning needle also works.) After drawing the outline of the leaf, place the paper on a hard surface and press the metal into the paper where you want the veins to be. When you shade over the indentations, thin, white lines will appear. (Practice this on scrap paper first.) For the texture of the leaf, I use the reverse burnishing method described on page 7, using a hard 2H chisel-point lead to apply one layer and then a softer F lead to apply another layer in a random, circular motion. A light touch of tacky eraser brings out the highlights, and the battery eraser adds light flaws.

Oak Tree Bark Oak tree bark is deeply furrowed. It is enjoyable to follow the interesting patterns and flow of the bark. To draw this bark, I use a 2B lead, followed by 4H and 2H chisel-point leads to create the even midtone shadows.

Drawing Leaves

How do you create the illusion of leaves without drawing every leaf? Simply concentrate on the shadows and textures and not on the individual leaves. Define the leaves by filling in the areas around and between them—this is called "negative drawing." Below is a three-step illustration that shows my method of drawing leaves.

Step 1 Using the underhand grip and the scribbling pencil stroke allows me to create controlled marks on the paper. This first layer is a general shaping of the tree and leaf bundles. I identify and sketch the branches that are not hidden by leaves.

Step 2 I start building layers, slowly working my way from the darkest shadows to the lighter areas.

Step 3 With each layer, I add more definition, texture, and structure to the leaf bundles.

Draw branches in key places

Open sky between branches is negative space

Four value layers

Drawing Foliage When drawing a tree in full foliage, squint your eyes to generalize the shapes and shadows so you can concentrate on the texture and overall shape of the leaf bundles. The distance of the tree—background, middle ground, or foreground—determines the amount of detail to include. The direction of your light source will determine the highlights and shadows.

Placement of Trees in a Landscape

The placement of a tree in a composition—whether it's in the foreground, middle ground, or background—will dictate how much texture and detail to include. As you learned on page 13, objects in the distance become smaller and less detailed. When depicting a distant object, provide just enough shape and detail to give the viewer the necessary clues to identify the object. Middle-ground objects should have more detail, but some aspects should be suggested rather than intricately depicted. Overall shape and lighting are important features to concentrate on at this viewpoint. Foreground objects should have the most detail, as these are closest to the viewer and offer the most information.

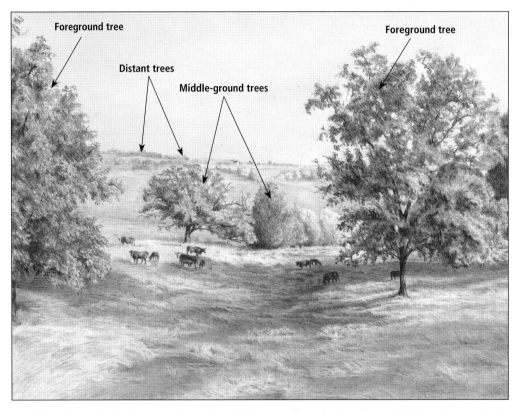

Depicting Distance Study this scene to understand how to depict trees at different viewpoints. The trees in the far distance are light with very little detail, whereas the trees in the middle ground have more detail; however, most of the branches aren't visible, and the trees have only a slight texture. The foreground trees have the most detail—the individual branches in shadowed areas add interest and provide depth, form, and shape.

SKIES AND CLOUDS

"There aren't any clouds in the sky, so why should I shade it?" I used to ask myself. Many of my earlier works do not include a toned sky. But I have learned that adding values to the sky broadens the range of tones available in a drawing. The white of the paper can be used to represent highlights or sun-kissed areas. A sky tone lends uniformity to a composition, adds a sense of reality, and provides atmosphere. Don't underestimate the importance of the sky, as it offers many moods that will impact the feeling of your drawing. Whether they're soft and misty or dramatic and cumulous, I create clouds by following the four-step progression shown below.

Backlighting This tropical sunset scene is a wonderful example of backlighting. The sky grows lighter as it approaches the horizon, and the clouds are backlit as the sun sets.

Step 1 I lay down a light layer of crosshatching using an F or B lead. Using the loose-hold grip and allowing the weight of the pencil to determine the pressure of the pencil stroke creates an even layer. I crosshatch three to five layers.

Step 2 I use a chamois in a light, circular motion to create a smooth, even base, taking care to avoid overburnishing the paper. (Flattening the paper fibers will prevent building additional layers of graphite.)

Step 3 After the sky is blended smooth, I use a plastic eraser and sculpt out the clouds. Then I use the tacky eraser to create soft edges for the wispy clouds.

Step 4 Now I layer graphite and blend with a tortillon to build up the cloud formations. When I have completed the sky area, I use a plastic eraser and a T square to clean up the edges and borders.

COMPOSITION

Up to this point, we have explored drawing basics and discussed the separate components of drawing landscapes. Now, how do we put it all together to create a pleasing composition? The simplest compositional decision to make is what to include and exclude from your landscape. Ask the question, "Is it just dead space, or does it contribute to the drawing?" Decide what to emphasize and what to leave less detailed. If all the elements are drawn with the same level of clarity and detail, they will compete for the center of attention. Many of my drawings are created using the "it just feels right" method. If it is pleasing to the eye, it usually works.

Is there a magical size to draw landscapes? If there is, I haven't discovered it yet. There is one important factor to consider when determining the size of your drawing: How detailed do you want your landscape to be? If the drawing is too small, the individual elements may be proportionately so small that you will not be able to capture anything but a hint of each element. That may be okay, but it needs to be considered before you start drawing.

Landscapes usually fall into three categories: close-up studies, middle-ground scenes, and panoramas. Close-up studies usually explore one subject's shape, proportions, details, and textures. Middle-ground scenes focus on the foreground objects, foliage, and structures, exploring the relationships among them. (I find that many of my landscapes fit in this category.) Panoramas are about space, vistas, mountains, seascapes, and rolling hills. Aerial perspective and composition are strong components of panoramas, as is the placement of the horizon.

Whichever elements, format, and size you choose, remember that you don't have to be a slave to your reference. That's the beauty of *artistic license*—the freedom to draw what you want to draw, even if it's not really there!

Taking Reference Photos

For many of us, drawing on location is not a practical option. However, if you get the opportunity, it is the most ideal situation. Feeling the breeze and the warmth of the sun and absorbing your surroundings while drawing on location helps you develop a relationship with the landscape, which is a most enriching experience.

The next best thing to drawing on location is to take your own photographs. Carry your camera with you all the time and don't hesitate to take pictures. With the availability of inexpensive digital cameras, taking photographs is an accessible and rewarding source of inspiration for the artist. Once you start envisioning and composing drawings through your camera lens, I guarantee that your view of your little corner of the world will never be the same. But don't feel that you have to take a professional-quality photograph. Your intent is to get reference photos to assist you when you are back at home.

When I've found an interesting landscape, it is not uncommon for me to take 100 to 300 photos from every possible angle. From all those shots, I might end up with just one or two that make it to the drawing board. I may go back to a site multiple times to capture a different angle, time of the day, or weather condition. But even if I still don't have the perfect photo, I can use photo-editing software or my imagination to tweak my reference, turning it into a pleasing composition (see "Manipulating Reference Photos" below).

When I am happy with my reference photo, I print two copies—one in color and one in black-and-white—at the size my drawing will be. I draw from the color printout and use the black-and-white printout to analyze values. Before starting my drawing, I make quick "thumbnail" sketches to study the values (see "Studying Values" on page 60).

Manipulating Reference Photos

If you are new to drawing landscapes, don't hesitate to follow your reference photo without changing the composition, as this is a great tool for learning how the elements all relate and come together. But once your skills have developed, you'll discover that finding a reference photo that doesn't need adjusting is a rare occurrence. Most photos will require some modification or compositional adjustment before you start drawing. Before the age of the computer, thumbnail sketches were the artist's best friend. Now there are additional tools for making this process better and quicker.

Your creative and artistic license can form an exciting partnership with photo-editing software. You can crop, merge, layer, lighten, darken, and even completely change a composition. Sometimes it takes just a little tweaking of a photo to create pleasing results, as shown in the example on page 21.

Weak Compositions Both of these photos are compositionally weak. In the photo at left, the most interesting element—the barn—is barely visible, and in the photo at right, there is no definite focal point—the barn competes for attention with the tree in the foreground.

Photo-Editing a Composition Using photo-editing software, I combine the landscaping from the above-left image with the barn from the above-right image. I move the barn up, closer to the foreground tree. The edited image is much more compositionally pleasing.

Final Drawing The final drawing, based on the edited photo, forms an original composition in its own right. The foreground vegetation draws the eye into the picture and leads it to the focal point, the barn.

KIRKWALL HARBOUR BASIN

Fellow artist Jim Fogarty sent me this beautiful photo of Kirkwall Harbour Basin in Scotland. The buildings in the background and the water in the foreground make up two of the three distinct surface planes in this scene. These are secondary or supporting components of the drawing. The middle-ground plane containing the boats holds the detail as well as the central focal point.

Adjusting a Scene In the reference photo, the two boats in the center are the same size; to add a little more variation, I slightly enlarge and bring forward the one on the left.

Preliminary Sketch
With a 2H lead, I lightly sketch the outlines of the boats and buildings on a sheet of tracing paper. Then I transfer the sketch to smooth-finish Bristol paper as described on page 4. I use an HB pencil and take care not to use too much pressure, as I don't want to leave any hard lines on the art paper.

Step 1 I use the retracted metal tip of a mechanical pencil to indent lines into the paper where two thin anchor ropes string across the fronts of the boats. When I shade over them later, they will remain white. (See "Oak Tree Leaf" on page 16.) I shade the boat in the front center first, using an F .5 mm mechanical pencil and strokes that follow the curves of the hull. Focusing on the cab, I lightly sketch the windows with a 2H pencil and a circular stroke, and I lay in some shadows with a 4H lead. Then I use a tacky eraser to lift out window reflections, and I create the general shapes inside.

Step 2 I shade the front left boat using the same method as in step 1 but with lighter values and less pressure. Then I move to the second boat from the left in the back row, which has wire mesh at the back that is lighter than the background. I use a form of indenting here: I take a 6H .5 mm mechanical pencil and draw each line of wire with firm pressure. Then I use a B lead and shade over it. The wire mesh appears as a lighter value but not white like the anchor ropes in step 1.

Step 3 As I shade each boat, I concentrate on the negative shapes. This is the key to creating details in such small areas. I am not outlining the details but rather shading around the lighter sections. I start shading the background behind the railings, leaving the railings white. Then I use a 4H to lightly shade the undersides of the boat railings, making them appear cylindrical. Returning to the boats, I simplify some of the details and try to capture just enough so the viewer can interpret the rigging and fishing equipment on the boats.

Step 4 Next I finish shading the dock edging and pillars. (Much of this area was already laid in as I detailed the boats.) The dark background helps push the lighter boats forward. Now I take the time to ensure that the dock is straight and that the perspective is correct. Then I create the concrete sections of the dock, using an HB lead with a downward vertical pencil stroke. I lift out the highlights with a tacky eraser, build up the darkest areas between the pillars with crosshatching and a 2B lead, and add the dock flooring with horizontal strokes using a 2 mm clutch pencil with a chisel-point 2H lead. I also add the coiled ropes on the right side, using an H .3 mm mechanical pencil in the shadowed areas.

Step 5 For the building on the right, I use a T square to make sure the walls and window frames are vertical and straight. Then I render the solid, midtone grays using an F lead for the base layer, followed by a 2H burnished layer. I lift out the window reflections with a tacky eraser.

Step 6 I don't want to include all the details of the building in the background, as they would compete with the boats, so I leave the windows nondescript on the top and a bit more solid on the first floor, deciding to omit two windows. I use random crosshatching and a 2 mm clutch pencil with a chisel-point 4H lead for a stucco texture on the upper half of the building, switching to a 2H lead in the clutch pencil for the lower half. Slightly more pressure and more layers create light shadows on the walls. The lone human figure leaning on the railing along with the stone building at left provide just enough darks to counterbalance the building on the right. I shade the stone building first with a 2 mm clutch pencil and a 4H lead, followed by short, broad strokes with a 2 mm clutch pencil and a B lead.

Step 7 To create the foreground water, I use a 2mm clutch pencil with a 2H chisel-point lead and the rocking stroke described on page 12. For the shadowed areas of water near the boats, I use a 2 mm clutch pencil with a 2B lead. I leave the water with minimal reflections and waves so it doesn't compete with the boats. To emphasize the soft, hazy effect of the drawing, I gently fade away the edges of the drawing.

DEPOE BAY

Depoe Bay, Oregon, has to be one of the most picturesque views of the north Pacific coastline. My good artist friend Karen Hendrickson shared this spectacular view of her "backyard" with me. This particular scene stands out because of its unique lighting and clouds, as well as a perfect tide level. The dramatic lighting adds to the scene but also poses challenges. The backlighting of the clouds, the silhouettes of the trees, and the frontal shadows on the bluffs and rocks are interesting to capture.

Although simple in composition, this landscape combines all four basic elements of nature: the sky and clouds, with their soft, dramatic lighting; the pine trees, with their branches delicately silhouetted against the sky; the rocks, providing the angular and solid mass jetting out into the ocean; and the water, with its turbulent waves crashing against the rocks.

Using Multiple References This scene poses unique challenges—the main one being that the bluff's details are hidden in deep shadows. Luckily, Karen provided me with a few other views, each of which held missing pieces of the puzzle.

Preliminary Sketch My preliminary sketch, made with a 2H pencil and very light pressure, helps me decide how to approach this seascape. I am mainly concerned with the rock formations and their placement.

Step 1 As I transfer the sketch to my art paper (see page 4), I use very little outline; I'm concerned primarily with the placement of the horizon and bluff. I lay in the sky as described on page 19, using a B lead for the first layer of crosshatching. After blending with a chamois, I begin to sculpt the clouds with a white plastic eraser. To keep the white edging of the clouds lighter, I layer the darker frontal puffs with an F lead, burnish them smooth with a tortillon, and then gently lift out the edges and the lighter, wispy clouds at the top center with a tacky eraser. I keep the clouds closest to the horizon small and compact to add aerial perspective. I give the clouds a smooth touch with a light layer of 2H, burnished with a tortillon.

Step 2 The line where the sky meets the water plays a critical role in the success of this drawing. The sky lightens just above the horizon, and the water edge at the farthest distance is slightly darker—these are subtle but important gradations of value. I draw the horizon using short, horizontal strokes and an F .5 mm mechanical pencil. I avoid using a continual pencil line, as this would create too strong a break between the sky and the water. I create a fine texture for the distant water, steadily increasing the detail and definition of the waves as I approach the middle ground. I overlap and layer my strokes to create a consistent texture. For the larger waves on the left side, I exaggerate the rocking motion. Then I shade the undersides of the strokes. I leave the white of the paper to represent where the strong glare of the sun reflects off the surface of the water.

Step 3 Because the trees form a dark silhouette, it is important that each branch is carefully placed. I practice my pencil strokes on sketch paper before I commit them to the actual drawing. I create tiny, irregular strokes with a .3 mm mechanical pencil and a 2B lead to create a rich, dark value. Varying the weight of the strokes is important to create the appearance of trees. I avoid creating a solid black layer, as this would result in a flat-looking area. The white spaces between the trees are as important as the branches in conveying the proper illusion of trees. I draw the grassy bluff, merely suggesting the grass as it hangs over the bluff edges.

Step 4 The sheer bluffs are eroded soil, not rock. I shade these using an F .5 mm mechanical pencil. I make the pencil strokes horizontal to indicate the various sedimentary layers, but I leave the bluffs fairly general with few details. The rocks projecting to the left of the bluff are dark and mostly in shadow. I make them lighter than they are in the reference photo to create more interest, and I detail the crevices.

◄ Step 5 As I progress through each rock formation, I start with the general shape of the overall rock and then incorporate angular planes to represent the various angles of the rocks in shadow. Each plane has its own reflective shadow and will vary based on the amount of light being reflected. I use an HB .5 mm mechanical pencil to shade the rocks. The softer lead creates a more grainy texture; I soften this by burnishing a top layer of graphite with a 4H.

Step 6 I detail the rocks, emphasizing crevices and subtle variances while maintaining the rocks' rugged appearance. By burnishing the distant rocks, I create a midtone value without sacrificing any detail. I darken the underbrush area in the pine trees to create more contrast. To capture the waves splashing onto the rocks with all their fluidity and turbulence, I use a battery-powered eraser and cut through the graphite with an upward stroke, lessening the pressure as I reach the tips of the waves. I subtly shade underneath each wave with an F .5 mm mechanical pencil, leaving the top edges of the waves lighter. The whitecaps appear as I draw the darker shadowed areas. The rocks that aren't yet underwater are flat with strong shadows. When I add the foreground waves, I reflect the swirls they create in the water.

Step 7 Next I shade the foreground waves using an F .5 mm mechanical pencil. The shading is stronger in the foreground, and the waves are larger. This accentuates the sense of depth. I use the battery-powered eraser to lift out additional waves crashing into the rocks. Some graphite smudging occurs, but I am able to soften this by applying a light layer of 4H lead over these areas. I pencil in the small, dark, shadowed areas just under the waves hitting the rocks, giving them extra contrast. I place a finishing layer of 4H lead underneath the waves. The impressionistic and less-detailed approach used in this drawing mirrors the feeling that I have only captured a momentary blink of the many different faces this location reveals on a daily basis. I can see this area being the foundation of many studies, exploring the limitless facets and possibilities provided by the time of day, the season, and weather conditions.

Transferring with the Grid Method

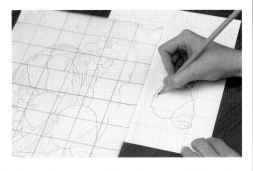

Another way to transfer a sketch is to use the grid method. First draw a grid of squares over the reference photo. Then lightly draw a corresponding grid over your drawing paper; the reference and your drawing paper must have the exact same number of squares, so even if they're not the same size, the original image and the drawing paper must have the same proportions. Once you've created the grids, simply draw what you see in each square of the reference in each square of the drawing paper. Draw in one square at a time until you have filled in all the squares. One-inch squares are great to start with, but just remember that the larger the squares, the more freehand drawing is required.

SONOMA DESERT

Marilyn Lavery-Corliss shared this unique desert scene with me. The landscape contains three distinct areas: the distant mountains, the bramble bushes and cactus in the middle ground, and the smaller cacti in the foreground.

▲ **Exploring Texture** With the sharp, spiny cacti and the thorny brambles, this desert scene offers a unique opportunity to experiment with different textures.

◄ **Preliminary Sketch** I use a 2H lead to sketch the composition onto a piece of tracing paper. By repositioning the cacti, I can tighten up the placement of the main elements. Introducing two desert quail to the right of the foreground adds interest to the scene.

Step 1 After transferring the sketch, I create the sky tone by lightly crosshatching three layers using an F .5 mm mechanical pencil over the entire sky area and then blending with a chamois. Then I use a plastic eraser to lift out white streaks to represent the wispy clouds. I carefully lift out the cacti areas against the sky, and I lightly shade the background mountains with a 2 mm clutch pencil with a 2H lead.

Step 2 Moving to the middle-ground area, I fill in the tall cacti with long, smooth strokes of a 2 mm clutch pencil with a chisel-point H lead. The upward motion of the strokes drawn for the shadowed areas is all I need to represent these tall cacti. I lightly draw the coarse foliage that surrounds the tall cacti. Short, dark cast shadows fall to the left side of the cacti.

Step 3 Next I work on the foreground elements, using a B .5 mm mechanical pencil. I use short, jagged strokes to represent the rough nature of the stems on the briar bush. Sparse, coarse foliage accentuates this bush.Using softer HB and B leads, I shade the large foreground cactus with short, angled pencil strokes that radiate from its dark center and seams.. Next I quickly shade the cluster of medallionlike cacti, filling in the shadows the individual pads cast upon each other and randomly placing just a hint of spines. Then I develop the quail (see "Quail Detail" below right).

Quail Detail When shading the quail, I concentrate on making sure the birds are the proper size and have the correct proportions. I am careful not to make them too detailed so they are well camouflaged in their surroundings.

Step 4 Using the same pencil, I add short, dark shadows to the foreground rocks. These accentuate the strong sunlight that is characteristic of a desert landscape. I place short patches of thin desert grass around the rocks, and I lightly shade the cacti in the foreground corner. I keep this area of cacti less detailed so they don't detract from the focal cacti. After making a few adjustments, my desertscape is complete.

FORT OF OUR LADY OF LORETO OF THE BAY

An artist friend, Nick Dynis, was kind enough to share a photo of this beautiful fort, Our Lady of Loreto of the Bay in Goliad, Texas. Despite the seemingly flat frontal view, shading can bring out the building's three-dimensionality. The differences between the stonework on the wall and on the building, as well as the tonal values and the perspective, are key components in making this view successful.

▶ **Emphasizing Textures** This simple composition can become a beautiful landscape scene by emphasizing and contrasting the rich textures of the stone walls.

Step 1 Because this composition is relatively simple, I start drawing directly on my art paper, rather than transferring a sketch. On a sheet of smooth-finish Bristol paper, I use a 2H lead to outline the basic architectural details of the building, using a ruler for the octagonal window. Next I block in the sky as described on page 19, using an F .5 mm mechanical pencil for the three layers of crosshatching. After blending with a chamois, I use a tacky eraser to drag some light, wispy clouds through the blended gray tone. I erase the excess graphite from the borders and from where the graphite has overlapped the building structures.

Step 2 For the stones on the building, I make random vertical and horizontal strokes with a variation of 2H and H chisel-point leads in a 2 mm clutch pencil. I lighten some areas with a tacky eraser and shade the building edges. I create the stones on the surrounding wall with a 2 mm clutch pencil with both H and HB chisel-point leads, using random crosshatch strokes to give individual values to each stone and leaving a small space between each stone and its neighbors. I burnish these lighter areas with a 2H lead. After I complete a section, I drag a tacky eraser through several stones. Then I use an H lead to make them less defined.

Step 3 I delicately shade the bell, the statue, and the octagonal window with a 2H .3 mm mechanical pencil. Then I continue to shade the stones on the face of the building and the surrounding wall.

Step 4 With a B .5 mm mechanical pencil, I draw each palm leaf with one stroke, starting at the center of the branch and drawing outward with an arcing motion and letting up on the pressure as I reach the end of the leaf. I leave a lot of open space between the branches. Then I shade the small bushes using a 2 mm clutch pencil with an H lead. A single dark edging on each leaf helps to define the undersides. I adjust the shading of the top edges of the building and the stones along the roofline. Next I draw the grass using short, upward strokes. Different tones and bare spots add variety and texture to the grass. The strokes are smaller near the building and increase toward the foreground area.

HOUSE PORTRAIT

Many homeowners enjoy drawings that capture the beauty of their homesteads and all the memories that they invoke. After talking to the owner of a house I wish to draw, I try to channel the homeowner's pride and enthusiasm into my drawing, as my goal is to capture the essence of the home. This house, a beautiful Queen Anne Revival, was built in the late 1890s.

Creating a Mood The close cropping of the house creates an intimate setting for this quaint scene; the porch invites the viewer right into the drawing. The tree arching over the front of the house and its strong cast shadows are added bonuses to this charming composition.

Step 1 After transferring my sketch of the house and foreground vegetation to smooth-finish Bristol paper, I use a 2 mm clutch pencil with a 2H lead to add just a hint of trees behind the house. I create the darkest part of the porch with a 4B .5 mm mechanical pencil. I switch to 2B and B leads as the tone of the porch supports lightens. I apply smooth, even shading inside the porch so there aren't any visible pencil strokes. I lift out the areas where the sunlight is cascading across the surfaces using a tacky eraser. I use a T square to make sure the doorjamb is perpendicular and straight, but I lightly draw the lines and then freehand over them. I don't want the perfect straight and rigid lines created by the ruler but rather the softer, less precise lines that freehand drawing provides.

Step 2 Light and shadow are not the only aspects that determine the tone of an area—color is a consideration as well. The gable of this house is a dark green that becomes a rich, dark value when seen in black-and-white. I usually draw from color photos for this reason and use a black-and-white reference only to match values. To capture the tone of the gable, I shade it with heavier pressure. Then I use a 2 mm clutch pencil with an H lead to block in a light layer of graphite on the rest of the house. I begin to lay in shadows on the roof and fascia with 2B and HB leads. Using a battery-operated eraser, I lift out the areas where the fascia is splashed with sunlight, softening up the edges of the erased sections with a light touch of graphite.

Step 3 I suggest the bricks with horizontal strokes, using a 2 mm clutch pencil to burnish a softer 2B lead over a harder 6H lead, creating an uneven texture. I add just enough detail to give the impression of bricks. Next I use heavier pressure and an H lead to add more of the shadows cast by the branches and leaves. The key to making realistic shadows is to make them conform to the underlying object so they become a part of it. I keep the window treatment simple—only an impression of window edgings and curtains is needed. I use a 2 mm clutch pencil with an H lead to create a smooth surface for the windowpanes and then add shadows from the tree branches with an HB lead. I lift out reflections using a tacky eraser. Then I draw the bushes and plants by shading the negative shapes around them with an HB .5 mm mechanical pencil. I lightly shade the centers of the plants with a 2 mm clutch pencil and a 2H lead, leaving the tips lighter to show that they are in direct sunlight. I use a 2B .5 mm mechanical pencil to draw the darker plants in the background with scribble strokes.

Step 4 The old oak tree adds a lot of character to this scene. The grooves in the oak bark are strong. Without drawing every groove, I am able to create enough texture to give the impression of the rough nature of the bark. I achieve this by using a 2B .5 mm mechanical pencil. I make the grooves in the bark closer together at the edges where the bark wraps around the tree. This provides the general three-dimensional cylinder effect of the tree trunk. I lay down the overall shading of the trunk using a 2 mm clutch pencil with an HB lead. Then I begin touching in shadows to the bush at the base of the tree.

Step 5 When shading the branches of the oak tree, I use a 2B lead, keeping in mind that the branches are stocky and angular. I pay careful attention to the joints of the branches, also remembering that the bark is rough and visible even on the smaller branches. With an F .5 mm mechanical pencil, I continue to apply consistent shading on the underside of the branches to create a uniform light source.

Step 6 Using the steps on page 17 and an F .5 mm mechanical pencil, I create the leaves. The branches remain largely visible with just a few overlapping bundles of leaves. I also add a darker tone to the background foliage.

Step 7 I draw the remaining leaves in four stages. Holding a 2 mm clutch pencil with a chisel-point HB lead in the underhand grip, I lay down the general bundles and shading. Then I remove the lightest leaves with a battery-operated eraser. Next I define and shade the undersections of the leaves to get them to come forward on the page and add depth. Finally, I add just a touch of detail to give the impression of leaves. With the leaves now finalized, I add more tone to the background foliage to increase the contrast.

Step 8 After adjusting the trunk shadows, shading more of the plants and leaves, and deepening some of the shadows on the house, this intimate, inviting scene is complete.

MOLEN DE ADRIAAN

This is a picturesque scene of Molen de Adriaan, located in Haarlem, the Netherlands. My good artist friend Tonia Nales has graciously shared this photo from her hometown. This *molen,* or mill, was originally built in 1778 but burned to the ground in 1932. Seventy years later, the citizens of Haarlem restored it to its original beauty. Its graceful, spinning sails dominate the skyline along the Spaarne River.

The focal point of this drawing is the windmill, so most of the detail is located in this area. I use the rules of aerial perspective to fade the background elements into the distance.

Adjusting Atmospheric Conditions
Although the reference photo shows an overcast day, I alter the composition to include puffy clouds. A few clouds add interest to the drawing without overwhelming the scene.

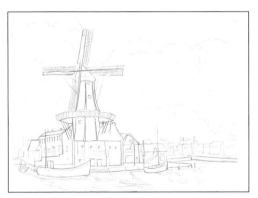

Preliminary Sketch First I use a 2H lead and sketch an outline of the composition on a piece of tracing vellum to work out the positioning of the buildings. Then I transfer the sketch to smooth-finish Bristol paper.

Step 1 Using an F .5 mm mechanical pencil, I lay down three layers of crosshatching on the upper two-thirds of the paper, keeping them smooth and even and extending them well into the areas designated for the windmill and other buildings. (It is far easier to erase excess areas of tone than to add tone later.) I use only two layers where the clouds are going to be. I use a chamois to blend to a smooth finish and then use a plastic eraser to "draw" the cloud formations. I darken the areas of the sky next to the whitest tops of the clouds using a 2H lead and then blend the graphite with a chamois. This adds depth to the sky and brings out the clouds. I repeat this process to slowly build up the clouds. I leave the sky fairly rough for a painterly, impressionistic look. I use a straightedge and erase a clean border around the image area. I also erase the edges of the windmill and buildings.

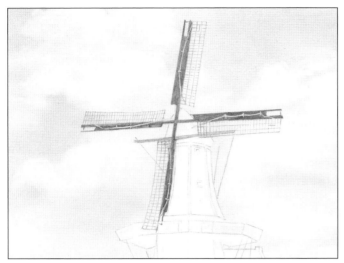

Step 2 I start detailing the armature and the sails of the windmill. I want these to be sharp and crisp, with straight angles, so I use a ruler to guide me. The fine mark of an HB .3 mm mechanical pencil is perfect for the thin lines of the sail's grid. The grid should not be the same line strength throughout, so I erase lightly here and there with a tacky eraser. This gives a realistic feel of the sun and sky bleaching out the details.

Step 3 I continue to use the HB .3 mm mechanical pencil as I shade the top of the mill. Using a B lead works well to render the dark structure, leaving the edges and windows white. The thin lead allows me to create crisp corners and edging in these small areas. The railed walkway forms an octagonal shape as it wraps around the building. I carefully shade the dark building behind the lighter boards of the railing. I draw the boards lightly where they overlap the sky.

Step 4 I shade the roof of the main building with short, downward-angled strokes using an HB .5 mm mechanical pencil. By concentrating on the varied tones, I make the shadows and textures appear. I build up the brickwork on the side of the building with short vertical and horizontal strokes, using a 2 mm clutch pencil with a chisel-point H lead. I draw the window openings with an HB lead, using a ruler to keep everything nice and straight. I take care to make the windows square.

Step 5 I develop the darkest areas under the dock to create the general form of the dock as it protrudes out into the water, using a B lead for the darkest areas and an F lead for the top of the dock. Because I am working only with tone, it is easy to carry over into the other objects and areas. I leave the boat on the right as a white shape to be completed later, but the development of the area around the boat on the left demands that I work the values of the boat, the dark shadows of the deck, and the water in one step. This is a technique that I use frequently. It is not drawing the objects separately that is important but rather the relationships of the tones and textures that separate the objects. I will return to the boat and water later to add more detail.

Step 6 I shade the buildings on the left with lighter values and fade them out in the background. I keep detail to a minimum; general shapes provide the impression of buildings. The buildings at right have a bit more detail in them as I identify the windows and staircase. I use a .5 mm mechanical pencil with an F lead on these buildings. I draw around the flagpoles and then lightly shade them using a 2 mm clutch pencil with a 2H lead. I keep the buildings and dock simple and leave out many of the miscellaneous crates and unknown objects that appear in the reference photo.

Step 7 I use aerial perspective to create depth in this scene, making the buildings in the background lighter and less defined. A few treetops, steeples, and chimneys form the skyline of the remaining backdrop for this majestic scene. General shapes of roofs and windows give the impression of buildings. Using a 2H .5 mm mechanical pencil, I shade the water next to the retaining wall in front of the background buildings. The water texture consists of small, horizontal, rocking strokes. I keep reflections minimal so the water doesn't compete with the sky.

Step 8 I continue creating the water in the foreground by slightly lengthening my horizontal strokes. Using an HB .5 mm mechanical pencil, I add the shadows and reflections made by the dock pillars as well as the reflections of the boats. To emphasize the aerial perspective, I adjust the values on the structures in the center, darkening the buildings and the surface of the dock.

Step 9 The water in the center foreground area has the darkest reflections from the windmill. I create these with an HB .5 mm mechanical pencil, placing the darks on the undersides of the waves. The diagonal line of the reflection leads the eye right into the scene. The highlights and shadows on the boats give them shape and form. Using an F .5 mm mechanical pencil, I add just enough details to the boats to fit them into the scene without drawing too much attention to them. They complement the scene, but the viewer's attention comes to rest on the beautiful splendor of the Molen de Adriaan.

HONEY CREEK

This peaceful, idyllic scene holds many wonderful childhood memories for me. Many hours of fishing and lying in the grass daydreaming and watching the clouds go by were spent "down by the creek." To me, this scene allows us to see nature at its finest.

This scene also is ideal compositionally. The gently winding creek leads the viewer's eye into and around the scene, and the large foreground tree on the left keeps the eye from straying off the page. The smaller trees in the distance give the appearance of depth and dimension, also leading the eye back into the scene.

Depicting Stillness This scene, with its mostly still water, provides a great opportunity to create a calm, quiet atmosphere. As you learned on page 12, you can represent still water by layering horizontal pencil strokes.

Step 1 Drawing directly on my art paper, I use a 2H lead to lightly sketch the bank and the shape of the creek—I don't sketch the trees yet, though. Next I lay in the sky with light tones that get progressively lighter as the sky reaches the horizon. Now I lightly sketch the outlines of the trees on top of the tone of the sky.

Step 2 Using the same pencil, I start building up the leaves of the distant trees using the progression shown on page 17. I use the underhand grip and the scribbling stroke, focusing on the mass of leaves as a whole. Next I shade the base of the foreground tree's trunk with an F .5 mm mechanical pencil, using short strokes to begin the grass along the creek.

Step 3 I continue using the F .5 mm mechanical pencil to shade the tree trunk and begin developing the branches. Once I've completed a few branches at the lowest part of the tree, I work on defining the focal point—the shadowed area under the foreground tree where the creek bends. I use my darkest tones here to really define this area, contrasting it with the light grasses that surround it. To create the patches of long grass near the bend, I build up layers of short pencil strokes. I use up-and-down motions to create these longer spikes (see page 12). I merely suggest the distant grass by hinting at the spikes. Then I start defining the distant curve of the creek by creating short strokes along the edges, making my strokes shorter and less detailed as the creek recedes into the distance. This is another good example of aerial perspective—objects in the distance appear less detailed and more blurry than objects in the foreground.

Step 4 Using an HB .5 mm mechanical pencil, I lightly sketch the grass along the banks of the creek. The grass closest to the water is broadleaf water grass, which nicely contrasts with the long, wispy weeds. For the grass in the foreground, I need to show enough detail to keep a sense of realism without drawing every single blade. To do this, I deliberately leave spaces among the weeds and overlap the layers. Next I use horizontal strokes to begin the water in the creek. Taking a break from the water, I start building up the leaves of the foreground tree, again using the steps from page 17.

Step 5 After creating the first layer of leaves in the foreground tree, I realize that the trees look too straight and perfect, so I make some adjustments. Still using the HB .5 mm mechanical pencil, I thicken the foreground tree trunk and put a slight curve in the trunk of the middle-ground tree, making it lean to the right a bit. I also make some small changes to the trunks of the background trees. I lift out the graphite with a tacky eraser and then use a kneaded eraser to make my changes. (Using an eraser without first lifting the graphite will grind the graphite into the paper—by lifting first, you can save the paper's tooth.) Now I develop the leaves of the middle-ground tree, and then I gradually darken the leaves of the background and foreground trees. I also start creating the grass and foliage of the hill on the left. Then I refine the grass on either side of the creek and continue to develop the water with horizontal strokes. I add a few rocks in the creek in the near foreground.

Step 6 With the same HB .5 mm mechanical pencil, I continue to shade the background trees, making them appear more three-dimensional. I make sure all the cast shadows fall to the right of the trees, showing that the light source is coming from above and left. Even the shadows of the grass are tilted to the right. I continue developing the water, making it darkest in the middle of the creek to show the shadow cast from the foreground tree. I also pull out some highlights in the water near the foreground grass to show its reflection in the water. I make some quick strokes around the rocks in the water to show the water's movement. Then I work on the grass on the left bank.

Step 7 Returning to the sky, I use a tortillon to darken the tone of the sky and reshape the clouds. When I'm satisfied with the shape and volume of the clouds, I concentrate on bringing out the textures of the grass and water. I add layers of grass to both sides of the creek, using longer strokes in the foreground and shorter strokes as I reach the middle- and backgrounds. I deepen the tone of the water, defining some of the rocks and curving my strokes around them to show movement. I lift out some highlights in the water to show the reflections of the grass. Then I return to the trees, using a 2B lead to darken areas and define the leaf bundles. I add small details to the foreground tree leaves, pulling out highlights in some of the leaf bundles to make them stand out. Lastly, I refine the foreground grass, making the grass closest to the creek darker and more detailed.

A MINER'S GLORY

This old mine structure (called the Lawson Headframe) is part of the Ontario Heritage Silver Trail. In the early 1900s, the mine was the largest producer of silver in the area. Located near the town of Cobalt, Ontario, Canada, it is considered by the local townsfolk a monument that represents the triumphs and hard work of the miners. Fellow artist Julie Brown sent me a number of beautiful Canadian scenes, but this mine framework really captured my attention. Of course, my love of dereliction (old barns especially) has a lot to do with it, but the close-up shot of the building, the unique structure, and the strong angles of the collapsing framework give an almost abstract feeling to the scene.

Contrasting Values This landscape provides a great opportunity to see the impact of drawing a white building against a toned sky.

Preliminary Sketch First I use a 2H lead and very light pressure to draw the composition on a sheet of tracing paper. I notice that the triangular shape of the building creates a strong composition and balances the top window and the two openings in the front of the building. The collapsing framework helps guide the viewer's eye in a circular motion around the picture plane. I use a straightedge to check the angles and perspective; then I transfer the drawing to smooth-finish Bristol paper.

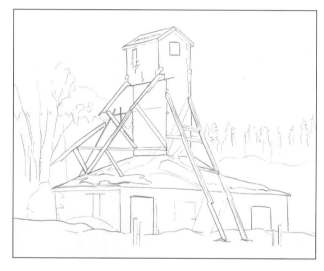

Step 1 I start with the sky, giving it a darker value than the photo reference. This allows for a wider range of values. If the sky is too light, the whites and highlights will not be as dramatic. I begin by laying down three layers of crosshatching with an F .5 mm mechanical pencil. I use the loose-hold grip and make the crosshatching as smooth as possible. Once this is completed, I use a chamois to blend until the graphite is smooth. I apply two more layers of crosshatching and blend them smooth. For the last layer of crosshatching, I use a 2H .5 mm mechanical pencil.

Step 2 I use a plastic eraser to make the blended edges of the building nice and crisp. I also use the eraser to create the negative shapes of the tree line. There is some lens distortion in the reference photo, so the sides of the building need straightening. When making this adjustment, I freehand the outlines to make the framework less rigid. I use a 2H .5 mm mechanical pencil to re-outline the building and armature. I closely compare the reference with my drawing, as the joints and angles seen in the photo provide the necessary clues to getting the angles and perspective correct.

Step 3 I start shading the top roof with an F .5 mm mechanical pencil, using short strokes that follow its slope. I add the light shadows under the eaves using a 2 mm clutch pencil with a 4H lead. I leave the paper white where the reflection of the sun is the strongest, just under the front window and along the right edge. Using a 2 mm clutch pencil with a 2H lead, I give the left side of the building a smooth layer of shading to provide an even shadow. I randomly add nicks and chips with an HB .5 mm mechanical pencil, and I use an F .5 mm mechanical pencil to add strokes indicating the imperfections on the individual boards. With an HB lead, I shade inside the windows, leaving slightly lighter areas inside them to add mystery. I draw the windowsills in shadow to add depth. I begin shading the supports using an F lead burnished with 6H.

Step 4 I work my way down the building, using a clutch pencil with a 2H lead for the base, an F lead for imperfections in the wood, and an HB lead for the darker shadowed areas. I draw the shadows that the armature casts onto the front side of the building with strokes that go in the direction of the boards on the building. I also make sure the imperfections and details overlap into the shadowed areas. (These two techniques help make the shadows sit on the building properly and look believable.) Cast shadows are important but should remain a supporting feature so they don't dominate the scene. I continue shading the supports using the burnishing method (see step 3).

Step 5 After continuing to burnish the supports, I shade the roof of the main building with an HB .5 mm mechanical pencil, leaving it fairly rough. Some of my individual pencil strokes are visible, but these provide the rough texture that I want. Again, I take care with the cast shadows to ensure that they follow the curves of the roof. I leave some areas of the roof completely white to depict snow, except for a few lightly blended areas to depict the snow's form and shape. I do this by lightly shading with a 2H and blending with a tortillon. I place small, dark shadows under the curves of the snow.

Step 6 I finish burnishing the supports before starting to shade the front of the building. I use a 2 mm clutch pencil with a 4H lead for the shadow under the eaves and accentuate the imperfections by adding nicks and chips to the building's surface. I shade the door openings, using a 2B for the darkest areas. With just a hint of pencil strokes on the edges and corners, a boarded window appears. I create the cast shadows that fall across the front of the building, making sure the details of the building overlap the shadows for realism. I don't finish the left side of the building yet because I want to incorporate the trees from the background into the shadows of the building.

Step 7 There are two types of trees that form two distinct layers in the background: Pine trees silhouette the sky, and birch trees surround the building. I start by roughly sketching the darker pine trees with an HB .5 mm mechanical pencil. I don't want a lot of detail. I use negative drawing, applying the darker pencil strokes between the trees first. I make short, upward pencil strokes (varying the pressure) to create the shadows between the trees and make the trees emerge on the paper. The birch trees are lighter, so I use a 2 mm clutch pencil with a 2H lead. I work from dark to light on these as well, leaving a few trunks white. I add shadows and dark notches on the birch tree trunks. With a 2B .5 mm mechanical pencil, I start developing the left side of the building, which contains the darkest values in the composition.

Step 8 Still using the 2B .5 mm mechanical pencil, I create even darker shadows on the left side of the building. I also add a couple of pine trees to the left of the building but purposely leave most of the area vague, eliminating much of the clutter. I lightly blend the shadowed areas of snow with a tortillon, allowing the white of the paper to represent the rest of the snow. With a 2H .5 mm mechanical pencil, I suggest the foreground fence by creating a hint of wire mesh—most of it is bleached out due to the strong sunlight reflecting off the snow. This helps create the illusion of a sunny winter day. I take a step back to view my drawing from afar and make a few small adjustments until I'm satisfied with the composition.

VENICE CANAL

I always enjoy when my co-worker Dave Neal goes on vacation—because when he returns he shares his photos with me, and I feel like I've been on vacation too. Venice, with its rich and beautiful buildings, is known as a home to artists. It is a real treat to draw the same subject matter many of the old masters have portrayed over the ages.

Even though they are in the foreground, the water and boats are secondary features. The gentle ripples and reflections of the water, as well as the placement of the boats, slowly draw the viewer into the picture plane. The sharply angled perspective directs the eye through the drawing. The buildings lead the eye around the corner. In contrast, the bridge directs the eye to the foreground and middle ground and prevents instant travel into the background and out of the picture plane. The most detail is applied to the focal point—the bridge.

Breaking Down the Composition
This photo is composed wonderfully, with the off-centered bridge, the depth and strong angles of the buildings, and the perfectly positioned gondolas. There are many fascinating details and rich textures. There is a lot going on in this scene, but by taking one section at a time, we can break it down into its basic compositional components.

Preliminary Sketch On a sheet of tracing paper, I use a 2H pencil and light pressure to block in the major areas of the scene, beginning with the buildings. These old buildings don't seem to follow a single perspective, as each has its own unique lean and angle. To force them to comply strictly with the rules of perspective will cause them to lose their character; however, some perspective needs to be followed to ensure that the buildings look logical and believable. I pay extra attention to verticals and the sharp perspective angles of the window openings. I add small details, such as the windows, but don't get carried away with them. I will attend to the details later in the drawing process. Next I sketch the bridge, the boats, and the water. When I'm satisfied with the drawing, I lightly transfer the lines to smooth-finish Bristol paper.

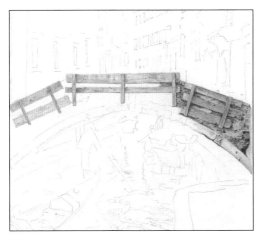

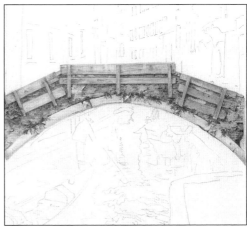

Step 1 I begin shading the old wood-and-brick bridge, keeping the right side of the bridge darker to contrast with the lighter buildings to the right while keeping the left side of the bridge lighter to contrast with the darker buildings on the left. I create the wood and brick textures as described on page 11. First I draw the outline with a 2H .5 mm mechanical pencil; then I shade the boards and add knots in the wood with an F .5 mm mechanical pencil. Next I burnish with a 6H pencil until I achieve an even-toned gray. Lastly, I make downward strokes with a tacky eraser to create highlights.

Step 2 The boards are worn and weathered smooth in comparison with the textured bricks, which contain dark areas in the corners and where the mortar has deteriorated. I use an HB .3 mm mechanical pencil and a thin, circular stroke that's perfect for the textured brick surface. A light layer of 6H gives the bricks a gray value that is slightly darker than the lower concrete bridge molding but lighter than the wood, resulting in a pleasing contrast of the three surfaces. I use a tortillon to smooth the curved concrete area edging the bottom of the bridge. I make tiny disjointed marks with an HB .5 mm mechanical pencil to depict the weeds growing out of the cracks.

Step 3 Now I add the sky to the background. Although it is tempting to leave the sky white, I give it a light value. As well as adding depth to the landscape, adding a value to the sky allows me to save the white of the paper for highlights. Using an F .5 mm mechanical pencil in the loose-hold grip, I turn my paper upside down and lightly lay down three layers of graphite. Then, using a chamois, I smooth the graphite, making it lighter as it approaches the buildings. Shading over the edges of the buildings ensures an even value.

Step 4 Now I begin to focus on the buildings on the right of the picture plane. Using random crosshatching with a 2 mm clutch pencil with a chisel-point 2H lead, I create a fine texture to represent the stucco on the buildings.

Step 5 I continue developing the buildings on the right, using the 2 mm clutch pencil with a 2H lead and a ruler to produce crisp edges as needed. When drawing realistic landscapes, it is not necessary to meticulously put in all the details. In fact, I find that the more I merely suggest the details (rather than drawing all of them), the more comments I get about how much detail I've captured! I put in only enough detail to hint at what is there—the viewer's mind fills in the rest (see "Suggesting Details" on page 53). It's not always easy to minimize the details, though—here I feel that I may have included too much detail on the balcony, so I'll try to counterbalance it by adding areas of detail on the left side of the picture plane.

Step 6 As I shade the buildings in the background with the same pencil as in step 5, I mainly concentrate on values, textures, and shapes. The more distant buildings receive less and less detail and appear almost blurry. I leave the white of the paper for the left side of the center background building to show that the light is hitting it. Now you can see the importance of adding a value to the sky—if I had left the sky white, I couldn't create the illusion of the sun hitting the center building without it looking washed out.

Step 7 Working from the detailed to the less detailed seems to be a good approach for these buildings. So I use the same method on the left side of the picture plane. I shade the dark corner just to the left of the bridge with a .5 mm mechanical pencil, using HB and F leads. Then I burnish with a 6H lead to give it a nice middle tone. Subtle hints of bricks and worn areas help add interest.

Step 8 The walls on the left side of the picture plane hold a host of wonderful details that I want to capture. Whereas I used 4H and 2H leads on the right, I start with an H lead on the left. The building beyond the bridge is darker because it is in shadow. I add details such as iron bars and railings to the top background window and another in the middle center. This helps counterbalance the ornate bannister on the right (shown in steps 5 and 6). A light pole attached to the building adds a pleasing detail. These details also provide good perspective keys.

Step 9 Having completed the background area behind the bridge, my focus shifts to the foreground. Because I included a few intricate details in the background, I will need to take additional care with details in the foreground. The left foreground building may not appear to have much detail, but I can create rich textures in the stucco. Careful to preserve the outline of the gondolier, I use the same random crosshatching I employed for the background but use a 2 mm clutch pencil with softer H and HB chisel-point leads. By using a tacky eraser and then re-applying softer and harder leads, I create a convincing texture. Next I add a drainage pipe running down the side of the building, and the watermarks at the base of the building begin to emerge.

Suggesting Details

When drawing the windows, I reduce them to two lines—one lighter, one darker—with a tad of a triangle on the top for shadows. This isn't much detail, but the results "read" as windows. The challenge is to render a window with sills, panes, edgings, etc., in terms of basic shapes. Understanding this concept is not as difficult as figuring out the key components that will allow the viewer to interpret an object as a window.

Step 10 Now I use an HB .3 mm mechanical pencil to shade the windows on the foreground wall and add the moss growing on the building. (The small lead is perfect for this detail work.) The plants and wrought-iron railing around the upper left window balance the composition. Next I use a 2B .5 mm mechanical pencil to shade the base of the wall, extending it into the darkest shadowed area under the bridge. Again, I preserve the outline of the gondolier as I shade the base of the wall. With the buildings finished, I move to the water and boats. Starting under the bridge, I use a 2 mm clutch pencil with a 2H chisel-point lead to shade the background gondolas and the water around them. With a B .3 mm mechanical pencil, I make the middle-ground gondola and gondolier a bit darker in value, also indicating more detail than I did with the background boats. Notice that the tip of the foreground gondola overlaps the middle-ground gondola. (I draw around the outline of the foreground boat to create the back end of the middle-ground boat.) Next I continue creating the water using the rocking stroke shown on page 12, alternating 4H and 2H leads.

Step 11 Still using the rocking stroke and a combination of 4H and 2H leads, I complete the water, making it look still and murky, almost oily. I leave patches of white to show the slight ripples that are created by the oars, but I add a slight value to even the whitest reflections—this will subdue the glare so it doesn't hold the viewer's attention. To add the reflection of the bridge in the right front corner, I apply a layer of graphite with an F .5 mm mechanical pencil and then burnish with a 2 mm clutch pencil with a 2H lead to smooth out the ripples.

Step 12 Now I use an HB .5 mm mechanical pencil lead and burnish with a 6H lead to shade the foreground gondola, the gondolier, his passengers, the objects inside the boat, and the oar. These are all supporting elements, so I reduce the objects and passengers inside the gondola to simple shapes, shaded only for depth. The viewer's eye recognizes these foreground elements, briefly gives them attention, and then travels back into the scene. A key approach to keeping objects fresh and not overworked is to apply the graphite at the correct value in the first layer. I do this by using just a few strokes for the objects within the boat.

Step 13 I realize that in giving the gondolier a different position from that in the reference photo, I have not compensated for the shifting of his weight and have ended up with an awkward figure. I try to resolve what doesn't look right. After some research, I decide that he needs to stand more upright, with his legs closer together. I also discover that most gondoliers stand on a swatch of fabric on the edge of the boat. I change his stance by first carefully removing the graphite using a tacky eraser. I switch to a white eraser, taking care not to damage the tooth of the paper. After redrawing the figure to my satisfaction, I finish the composition by making minor value adjustments to bring the entire drawing together: With a .5 mm mechanical pencil and a 2B lead, I emphasize the darkest areas of the drawing, such as the foreground boat, the upper left window shadows, and the shadows under the bridge.

ITALIAN COUNTRYSIDE

This Italian countryside scene is a great opportunity to try out subtle tones and textures. The scene is compositionally strong. The valleys divide the picture plane into a pleasing pattern. I will need to lighten most of the trees in this scene in order to achieve detail and a dramatic mood.

Observing Details This reference photo will allow me to observe details such as tree structure and shape, which will help me give my drawing the level of realism I am striving for.

Step 1 With a 2H lead, I start drawing a light outline directly on my art paper to lay out the general placement of the trees and valleys. Using the loose-hold grip and an HB .5 mm mechanical pencil, I use crosshatching to create an even tone for the sky. After smoothing the graphite with a chamois, I use a white plastic eraser to sculpt the cloud formations. Using an F .5 mm mechanical pencil, I lay in additional areas just above the white cloud tops. This provides contrast and crisper areas in the clouds. I shade the bases of the clouds as well. A dark cloud is descending over the top left corner and is backlit by a lighter area. I continue to sculpt and give form to the clouds by adding and removing layers of graphite. I make more subtle changes by lightly dragging a tacky eraser over certain areas, gently removing the graphite.

Step 2 | I shade the tree in the right foreground using the under-hand grip with an HB .5 mm mechanical pencil. Short, outward strokes create the impression of leaves. To make the tree realistic, I take special care to maintain open areas between the branches. To keep the area fresh and not overworked, I try to get the right tone with the first application of graphite. I press harder for darker areas and lighten the pressure for lighter areas to control the tones. Next I begin drawing the background slope and vegetation on the right.

Step 3 | I add hints of shadows to create the objects along the fence in the background. A small building is tucked among the trees on the hillside, and rows of grape vines lead the viewer's eye down the hill. The hay bales are quickly given form by their shadows. With a 2 mm clutch pencil and a 2H chisel-point lead, I add the lighter tone of the surrounding hay field. I start blocking in the even tone of the foreground grass using a 2 mm clutch pencil with an HB lead. Then I use an HB .5 mm mechanical pencil with short, up-and-down strokes to create the illusion of grass and weeds.

Step 4 | I continue to block in the grassy area and detail the grass. The weeds are clumpy, so I keep them uneven. I make the shading under the tree in the middle ground dark, and I draw the shadows behind the lighter weeds in front.

Step 5 I start working on the tree in the center, first shading the main branches and the trunk for placement. I study my reference photo carefully in order to capture the unique characteristics of the tree. I use an F .5 mm mechanical pencil with the underhand grip and a scribble stroke to give the first layer of leaf bundles a nice texture.

Step 6 I apply additional layers of shading to darken the shadowed inside areas of the tree. Working from dark to light, I give form to the branch bundles. I leave open spaces between the branches to define the tree and give it form.

Step 7 I leave the background trees undefined so the foreground trees maintain the focus. I shade the three poplar trees at left with short, upward strokes and a 2B pencil. Although it is tempting to create smooth, cylindrical forms, the reference shows me that the branches protrude out on the sides. The small open spaces between the trees, as well as the dark branches at their bases, are important details for drawing realistic trees.

Step 8 With a 2B .5 mm mechanical pencil, I create the hay field in the lower left corner of the landscape. I move the hay bale up into the picture plane just a bit. With the same pencil, I add a few rocks and some dirt in the lower left foreground corner to complete this lovely European landscape.

Smooth Skies

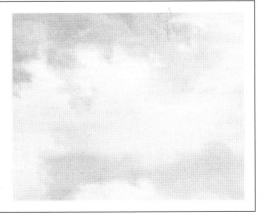

Sometimes, no matter how carefully you work at getting an area of sky smooth, the natural irregularities of the paper make it difficult. When this happens to you, simply use a tacky eraser to make very light, wispy clouds to hide any flaws. For a smooth finish, apply a final layer of crosshatching with a 2H lead and blend with a chamois. Wrap a chamois around a tortillon and blend to smooth out the small areas of sky visible behind the clouds.

BEFORE THE STORM

Landscapes can evoke strong emotions by setting an atmospheric mood. The effect can be subtle or dramatic—the choice is completely up to you. To me, this landscape depicts nature's battle between serenity and turbulence. The dark rain clouds competing with the bright sunlight creates a dramatic contrast of values.

This scene also holds special meaning for me, as it was originally drawn as a tribute to my father-in-law, John Wright, who at the time was battling cancer. This rendition is dedicated to the remembrance of his strong spirit.

Making Changes To create a more pleasing composition, I will make a few adjustments to my photo: I will tuck the foreground tree behind the barn to emphasize the focal point (the barn), add a dirt road to provide a visual path for the viewer, and place a plow in the foreground to keep the viewer's eye within the scene.

Studying Values

Here you can see that the darkest values are on the roof of the barn and the right side of the middle-ground tree. The middle values are in the bands of rain on the left side and on the dirt path. The lightest values are on the face of the barn and in the foreground grass. Preplanning the placement of your values will strengthen your composition by creating uniformity and balance.

Step 1 First I sketch the scene on tracing vellum. Because I'm adding the plow from another resource, I experiment with its placement until it fits naturally into the scene. When I've found a pleasing composition, I do a quick value study on scrap paper (see box at left). After transferring the sketch to smooth-finish Bristol paper, I lay down the first layer of the sky—I use an F pencil and the loose-hold grip to lightly crosshatch, darkening the tone in the sky's center.

Step 2 I continue crosshatching the sky area, keeping my strokes light and consistent. Then I wrap a chamois around my index finger and use light, small, circular strokes to blend until the tone is even and I can't see any individual marks. Once the sky is blended, I use a plastic eraser to lift out tone for the clouds. For lighter, softer cloud areas, I use a tacky eraser. Now I use a tortillon to burnish over the tops of the clouds and detail in the darkest areas where the sky and clouds meet. I am careful never to rush this process; I actually spend quite some time concentrating only on the sky. I extend the sky well into the areas designated for the horizon, trees, and barn. Now I take a harder 3H pencil to refine the sky, blending the tone to smooth it. Then I begin putting down the first layer of the foreground tree, following the steps on page 17. Using a B .5 mm mechanical pencil and the underhand grip, I start indicating the leaves with the scribble stroke.

Step 3 I use a 2B .5 mm mechanical pencil and crosshatching to create an even, dark tone for the roof of the barn. I use a much lighter touch for the side of the barn, making vertical strokes to represent the wood. I use a ruler to create the edges of the barn. Returning to the foreground tree, I shade the branches. Then I use a B .5 mm mechanical pencil and the underhand grip to add more scribbling strokes for the foliage. I work from dark to light, concentrating on the areas of shadow among the leaves. As the shadowed areas develop, the lighter areas also begin to form. I lightly drag my tacky eraser over the leaf areas to create highlights. I pay particular attention to the leaves at the edge of the tree, as these are the most distinct. To keep the tree realistic, I create an uneven pattern of foliage, leaving open areas so the branches are visible. For the lighter branches, I switch to a 2 mm clutch pencil with a chisel-point 2H lead.

Step 4 I continue developing the roof, using a ruler to create straight lines. For the barn's wood texture, I lay down a light, vertical layer of tone with an F pencil. I use heavier strokes to depict the grainy texture of the wood, and I use a B pencil for the darkest areas. Then I burnish a layer of tone with a 6H pencil on top and lift out highlights with a tacky eraser. Next I use the same steps as I did with the foreground tree to create the middle-ground tree, but I darken the tone where the tree meets the barn. I use the same scribbling strokes for the small bush near the barn door. For the middle-ground weeds, I use a 2B .5 mm mechanical pencil and quick, spontaneous strokes. Then I use short strokes and a 2 mm clutch pencil with a chisel-point H lead to start filling in the grass, being sure to preserve the plow handles. I accentuate the dark area of sky in the distance and create bands of rain by lifting out diagonal streaks with my tacky eraser. I also use long strokes to indicate a cornfield at the horizon.

Step 5 Using an F .5 mm mechanical pencil, I create the grass around the dirt path. The grass has multiple layers of texture, which I achieve by changing the direction of my strokes and erasing to create uneven, spontaneous lines. With a 2B .5 mm mechanical pencil, I form the worn path by gently blending my strokes in a U-shaped motion with a tortillon. Then I lift out highlights with my tacky eraser to depict the variations in the dirt. I go back over the grass again, making sure that the foreground grass has more detail and is darker in tone than the middle- and background grass. Next I use an HB .3 mm mechanical pencil to begin detailing the plow, keeping a middle-value tone.

Step 6 Once I'm satisfied with the wooden texture of the plow, I use additional horizontal strokes to finish the dirt path, creating a smaller dirt path that seems to lead to the plow. I do this by erasing a line of tone and then layering horizontal strokes over the erased area, using a 2B .5 mm mechanical pencil and the same U-shaped motion, blending with a tortillon. I detail a few more areas of grass, paying particular attention to the direction of my strokes. Notice that the grass on the right side of the picture plane is angled toward the right side of the barn, and the grass on the left side of the picture plane is angled toward the left side of the barn. The weeds on the left side of the picture plane, however, are angled to the left. These directional differences help lead the eye into and around the scene, making for a pleasing composition. Now I add another layer of shading to the barn's face and side. After a few more adjustments in tone, my landscape is finished.

CLOSING WORDS

I would like to thank Walter Foster Publishing for allowing me to share my passion for drawing with you. So where do you go from here? What's next? I'd like to recommend that you find a mentor to assist you or join an online art forum or local art group. "Sketch crawls" are held across the world. It is fun to share your drawings with other artists who enjoy the same medium and subject matter. The support and creative energy that you will receive from them is immeasurable.

I would like to thank my mentor, Mike Sibley of England. During these past few years while I regained my skills and confidence, he has been there to guide me. He is an incredible artist, author, and web designer, and my dear friend.

I also want to thank a special group called "DrawingTogether2." They are an online group of artists from around the world who share a passion for drawing. Through their support and "dare to imagine" attitude, they have stretched my imagination in many unbelievable ways, including the possibility of authoring a book. The world is a much smaller place because of them.

I want to thank several people for letting me travel and experience the world through their eyes and camera lenses. Their contributions to this book are really appreciated: Julie Brown (Canadian mine photo), Nick Dynis (Fort of Our Lady of Loreto of the Bay and stone bell photos), Jim Fogarty (Kirkwall Harbour Basin photo), Karen Hendrickson (Depoe Bay photo), Marilyn Lavery-Corliss (Sonoma Desert photo), Tonia Nales (Molen de Adriaan photo), and Dave Neal (Venice photo).

You can find me on the web and e-mail me through my website—I'd love to hear from you.

—Diane Wright